THE FIRST DEATH OF VENICE

Martin Stokes

THE FIRST DEATH OF VENICE

BLOODAXE BOOKS

ISBN: 1 85224 029 6

First published 1987 by
Bloodaxe Books Ltd,
P.O. Box 1SN,
Newcastle upon Tyne NE99 1SN.

Bloodaxe Books Ltd acknowledges
the financial assistance of Northern Arts.

Typesetting by Bryan Williamson, Manchester.

Printed in Great Britain by
Bell & Bain Limited, Glasgow.

'These came out through the white man's writing stick, down upon paper, and were sent away.'
PATRICK WHITE, Voss

Acknowledgements

Acknowledgements are due to the editors of the following publications in which some of these poems have appeared: *Argo, Chapter and Verse, Chester Poets 1987 Anthology, Context, Encounter, The Gregory Poems 1983-84* (Salamander Press, 1984), *Iron, Litmus, Maxy's Journal, Outposts, Oxford Poetry, Poetry and Audience, Poetry Durham, Poetry Review* and *Proof.*

Cover illustration by Irene Reddish.

Contents

Hubris, off the White Cliffs

Our bomber flying home
drops eight remaining bombs.
To see the water plume
she circles round the bombs.

For spectacle and noise –
REVERBERATING BOMBS –
she circles in the noise
and passes round the bombs.

A flight of Messerschmitt,
remembering the bombs,
fires at the plane and it,
in smithereens, like bombs

drops and makes another pass
across the pluming bombs.
The Messerschmitt then pass,
then leave the pluming bombs.

The Moehne Dam

'... another and intriguing way, thought Wallis
whimsically, of attacking the enemy at the source of
power.'

PAUL BRICKHILL, The Dam Busters

I.

A dam

defended by a heavy flak

emplacement, by searchlights,

and beautified

by ornamental pine trees.

A device designed high

and very thick, wide to withstand

stress, the pressure of its lake, C

and pierced to let out part O

of its catchment. Several pipes N

diverted water for the Ruhr foundrymen C

to drink and wash in. The volume of its depths R

rewarded summer mornings, afternoons, E

light evenings of quiet fishing, and maintained T

high levels for the long, slow, heavy barges E

heaving coal and iron through a network

of canals, delivering to foundries

for the manufacture of more tanks,

more locomotives, aircraft, guns,

more badges for distinguished service

and medals for acts of bravery,

such as bombing.

The vertical acrostic on the right reads: R A M P A R T

II.

One
hundred
and thirty-four
million tons
of water
gone.

C
O
N
E
T
E

R
A
M
A
R
T

Gone to flood the coal mines,
cover aerodromes, shut factories,
fuse the valley's hydro-electricity.
Water, pouring out, just gone
to damage forty-seven bridges
and re-align the railways.
The whole reservoir gone
to put its hands over bells and lights
and drown a thousand people
(half of them were allied troops
in a prison camp). Leaving behind
a smell of mudbanks, boats, inverted fish,
a pair of ring-necked whooper swans
and other nesting rare birds.

13

A Song Against the Romans

While both the Generals played check-mate outside
    Outside!
The soldiers stopped us with sarcastic threats
    Their threats!
They took our city, scoffing bread and wine
    Our wine!
The Generals then rode through the gates
    And said something, and ruled.

We threw down our defences on command
    Command!
And built them up a stronger city wall
    A wall!
But the enemy's already inside
    Inside!
We need protecting only from
    These heavy Roman troops.

    Since we ourselves have built it up
    We know how we can smash it:
    Our mason's own construction tricks
    Will help us bring it down.

They wanted straighter, harder roads than ours
    Than ours!
We laid them down and took to wearing shoes
    To shoes!
The yearly race is not so golden now
    Not now!
But we'll be running, storming through
    And win a better prize.

    We set the stones in rigid lines
    For them, for marching out:
    Their soldiers' column, Corinthian pillar,
    Straight minds and middle sewer.

We built an aqueduct to grow them fruit
    Our fruit!
The arches took their shape from our strides
    Our strides!
The buttresses from all our working arms
    Our arms!
They made us bring our hearth-stones
    When the sandstone quarry ceased.

One man refused to break his home for them
    Refused
And joked that water would fall off the bridge
    He joked
More often than our clever builders had
    They had
One night they drove a wheel spoke
    ('An accident') in his eyes.

    They sent him out to entertain
    Drunk soldiers in their tents.
    He suffered from his stoning-scars
    And the sheer fun of dogs.

They showed us how to build a richer tomb
    A tomb!
To bury him and others whom they killed
    They killed!
But we did not carve acanthus in the frieze
    Their frieze!
I told my men to cut the leaf,
    I told them, it was I!

    I am their demagogue: I speak.
    These words are not complete:
    There's going to be resistance soon,
    Scaring to our wives.

Up from being perilled to the floor
    The floor!
Out from our tunnels in the crust of earth
    Our earth!
And hard down on their power to the blood
    Their blood!
We'll spill it on their portraits
    And their profiles done in chalk.

The summer's yours, you Romans, yours again
    It's yours!
We sing the coming autumn will be ours
    Be ours!
We'll craft a vicious ballad when we've won
    We'll win!
And you'll be left so far away
    The echo will not reach.

A Croft Is a Small Holding

I promised to tell the truth and nothing, now,
but that declivity – doors kicked and soon
the slow destruction of our cottages,
ours and his, preceded (just) by summons
of removal. Long roofs dropping, smouldering
for days. Thick sods which made good thatch
returned to grass, prefiguring his sheep.

A shepherd now (or two) perhaps may steal
protection in the scarce lee of a wall.
The young and strong have died, or scatter – some
to cities in the south but most abroad
from motives of compassion to themselves.
The old majority and I remain.
We get the church door's sterling per annum.

My food was simple, now in the extreme.
I can live upon potatoes, fish and more
potatoes. I am able, now, and qualified
to plant potatoes in the earth so cold
it does not feel like a bed at all.
Outside my small holding I am able
to lie down, survive my strenuous sleep.

B

The Orders for the Massacres of Glencoe

1. *To Captain Robert Campbell of Glenlyon*

You are hereby ordered to fall upon
the rebels, the MacDonalds of Glencoe,
and put all under seventy to the sword.
I say you are to have a special care
the old fox and his crafty sons do not,
on no account at all, escape your hands.
You Campbells must secure all avenues
that no man escapes.

                This you are to put
in execution, friend, at five o'clock
precisely; and by that darkening hour,
or shortly after, I shall strive to be
beside you with a stronger field of men.
If I do not come to you at five,
do not tarry for me but fall on.

This is by the good King's special command
for the good and safety of our country homes,
that miscreants be cut off root and branch.
See that this is put in execution
without feud or favour, or else you may
expect to be dealt with as one not true
to King nor Government, nor a man fit
to hold commission in the King's service.

Thus expecting that you will not fail
in the fulfilling hereof, as you so pride
yourself, here I subscribe thee with my hand
at Balicholis, February 12th, 1692.

                           R. Duncanson.

2. *To the Sassenachs.*

Now look, I'm telling you to drive across
the lanes, the land, the customs of Glencoe
and frighten everybody young and old.
You must make sure the people and their farms,
their property, their shops and all their scenes
do not escape your wheels and heavy boots.
You shall march up each track and path and place
so that nothing escapes, and the ghouls shall gaze.

You are to start all this at 8 a.m.
on each fine summer day, and soon, by one
or very shortly afterwards, busloads
– day-trippers – will arrive and join you there.
If you don't meet them, then the forecast's bad
and you are not to go outside but stay indoors.

By the Scottish Tourist Board's command,
for the fame and livelihood of old Glencoe,
these innocents will not have house nor home.
See that this is carried out with friends
but with no favour, none, or else you will
be dealt with as poor Sassenachs not true
to us nor grand Glencoe, nor a man fit
to have his own vehicle in his own name.

Knowing that you will do as we command,
since all of you must visit Glencoe once,
I sign this leaflet with my hand and heart
at Edinburgh, February 12th, 1962.

Alan D. Toodear.

The First Death of Venice

I.

They skimmed a pebble out.
The rising tides absorbed it.

Our eldest men observed.
They questioned why our land grew waterlogged
despite the normal measurements of rain;
they questioned why our cultivated slopes
were losing excellence and yield,
and had become less steep.

For seasons, something too slow
to recognise deprived those rounded crests
of height. Our soils turned mud
descended to an undulating plain.

We thought of all our offshore isles
and sand-spits as harbour walls.
The fishing-scullers often took
our children to the beaches there:
until both shores became a marsh
and our crescent-curved lagoon
the wind's catapult.

High waters dug new creeks
into our privilege. Low floors grew moist,
walls dripped as fetid thriving moss
and lichen-root split planks, bit out
the weak calcareous mortar, then the stones.

In the cold dawn, when the sun
percolates the ground-mist and the fire-smokes,
the sea controls the land
as a queen dictates her serfdom.

We were living in the meantime.

II.

It rained for three days,
rained as if the summer's earth
had to be and would be swamped
beneath a cancellation into debt,
before the new year's winter could blow in.
Big thunder crackled, cracked
and spat aground against its brittle trees
of lightning, to induce emergency
across the premature dome-darkness.

The unknown storm –
burst from low pressure –
drove itself in bedrock.
Once at its union
with everything, it shrieked.
Full skies attacked my door
from where I listened and watched,
slammed it back and back,
sucked out hinges, shutter-wood.
I heard branches whistled off.
I saw a tangled fence, exhausted, fight.
I saw tiles slither, roofs.
I saw our small boats hit
and go, run over by the air.

Ruptured, my roots plucked out –
not quite tensile enough –
I felt I was a tree struck down,
a victim breath still blows about
and still finds poised. Held there by fun
a child's doll, twisted and distended, bound
in swinging branches, must have loved these games.

I fled. The power in the wind
could not be judged, and oil lamps
flashed warnings or flicked out.
I clambered over tiers
of splintered furniture, across
long tables, shelving, scrolls
of ancient letters worshipping the floor.

Behind me, waves of mud and stone
fell through my halls.

I ran along torrential streets
prayer-swung with citizens.
They chanted intercessionary pleas
for hope: when the beams and lamps collapsed
their voices writhed in charcoal.
Some others, wrapped in straw
as pale as themselves, put trust
in optimism. Down that glut
of black rain, one man simply stared:
Why are these ripples in the pool
aspherical?

III.

That tree is green and that one's green:
those trees are green. This place
is fit for cerebral decline.
And that's the sun, which I
desire, most desire. It is not here.
A solitary place, fit
for dreamers or for quipping blasphemy.

The swallow is my host.
A forest and a lake come to my door.
For mirrors, I have water. In it
my slopping mouth is smeared with berry-juice.
When am I acceptable,
living on this hill?
Not even in the public of the animals.

To look down on my town in ruins
is pointless. There is nothing, no one.
Nothing to see except
our feeding river, braided now
and shallow, and its new banks
composed of incoherent sediments,
spoons, money, ceilings, families
falling to the sea.

IV.

I am known to both sides
of the influencing moon.
I feel her success with me,
how she likens me to solitude,
withdraws sane speech from my tongue;
how she decays my clothes,
and insists that I stare back
until my face, too, is pocked.

I am her point of ridicule,
a fool to be dispatched about his room
on errands of thought. For months,
against her cold, steady will,
I have been trying not to meditate.
But my nights are sent revolving through long years,
and still my life is mine alone.

You, let me curse you, moon and sea,
let me curse you then repent;
repent, because you're agents who perform
the planet's natural flux and chance.
There were seditious liars in our town
who shouted in belief that sea and sky
were two performers of catastrophism,
come down to punish gross expansion, war,
the King's behaviour, and even simple trade.
Importance does wean jealous eyes
and callous minds: we had no more
in office than were needed for survival.

I was a trader, I owned fishing-boats.
I studied literature, and I subscribed
each time to our militia corps.
I have no guilt – why should I?
I sought work and pleasure; sought a life
dedicated to the most refined
exacting purpose that I knew.

I turn in sleep on this decree:
to love my city, Venice.
Ever since the first small colonies
there must have been, I feel it,
a passionate, ambitious creed
driven in Venetian generation,
and there is greatness still.
Be supplied by honour, and be strong.
Where is your heiress? Rise her gently up
and build her well. But do not wake her slowly –
years are not my friends and I might fall.
Already splinters pierce the mud,
wanting bastion. Ox-whips
imagine wheels, commerce and fresh food.
In my vision stones rejuvenate,
for Venice is no figment
of our history. My street
shall be a place I will have seen.

Swabian Castle
(for Klaus Fischer)

Built in mist on the precipice
for war, coat of arms of antlers. In the vale
he supervised the butchery,
in the high chapels, Catholic or other
(some were just converted look-out posts),
he mumbled prayers for peace

and territory. More acres yield
more grain. The rightful King at the armoury door
can take the air. The view is a fine one,
when the weather is clear, of fleeting peace:
subject people flourish, women till the battlefield
which hangs already in his study.

A watch on the rebel or courtly neighbour,
he feeds his father's library, taking dreams,
and tends to his mistress, drunk.
It's growing dark: they stay in bed
as heavy rain brings down more of the castle walls
than ever any army.

Natural Colours

'Artists in England are paid too much.'
PRINCE ALBERT

An aged shepherd, knotty crook,
by tranquil grove or shady brook;
a rainbow, hay wain, happy gaze,
perpetual windy fields, fine days;
the ruins are ruined and waterfalls don't fall;
definitive brushstrokes stroke them all
from ostentatious clouds to breathless dog,
the thousand-year-old shepherd whistling God.

The knotty shepherd – a crooked sheep –
he had no copyright to keep,
no royalties. So he began his own
life-drawing, one huge work, and his alone,
a work produced according to the rate
of each year's wage per ten square miles of gate
and realist wind, of monochrome rainbow,
of wetting mist and honest cold grey snow.

The Music of the Titanic

'O You Beautiful Doll' played out to them,
the ragtime lifting one foot
then the other off the carpet floor:
so the impact passed gently, unremarked.

On being woken by the stewards
and made to dress in life-jackets
some people who had tired of the dance
and gone to bed, went back to bed.

Already scores of immigrants had died,
disturbed by water in the lower decks.
A ship's engineer came up from there.
The Captain listened quietly to him.

At no request, no order,
Wallace Hartley stopped the melody.
His band – three violins, two celli, double-bass –
began a slow Episcopal hymn.

'God of Mercy and Compassion,
Look with pity on my pain,
Hold me up in mighty waters,
Keep my eyes on things above.'

No one sang the words of little comfort.
Not the wives and children cold or choked
in the bottom of the half-empty lifeboats,
neither men too stupid and polite to board.

Familiar or unknown to them,
they listened to the hymn tune again
as they stayed, or finally swam, or panicked
in the suction of the ship turning on end.

The musicians kept to the boat deck. The lights went
and machinery roared down through the ship,
through which the band continued playing.
No one knew how they were doing that.

The band still playing 'Autumn',
heard by men submerged but not yet drowned,
as the liner settled in a shriek of steam
and small cries in key.

The ocean came quickly, killing them,
then lifted the musicians from the ballast
of their instruments and laid them down, and laid down
their instruments and took them into care.

Water sealed the last pitch in each string
and held the hymn inside the belly and the wood.
What spread from the sound-holes
dulled the underwater edges of the ice.

A weak pulsating rhythm played,
attended to by fish before they left.
The pressures equalised throughout the hull.
They swam back up to depths where they survived.

The sea-bed – firm silt with no sea growths or rocks –
prepared its cushioning effect
and received the vessel upright like a coffin,
and the mourning-music, fainter but intact.

From under locked doors, down passageways,
diminishing chromatic lines seeped out,
up through the funnels, or over the ripped plates,
beginning journeys through the North Atlantic.

Deep currents dissipated, circled it,
and 'Autumn' still travels, making voyages,
performed continually in open score,
expanded, subject to repeated change.

Returning sometimes to its origin
the old, composer's scale is restored,
where overlapping figures of the hymn,
sustained by long-wave, guard the hull.

A diver salvaging the wreck would miss it,
but the music stays preserved less vulnerably
inside the ship itself, two miles down.
He wouldn't hear. It isn't meant for him.

He wouldn't feel it in the instruments,
it isn't anything he knows,
although it's there, sounding for the dead,
the owner, the Captain, any stowaways.

Down in an opened vault, it decorates
three crewmen round a jewelled Rubaiyat,
and fingers without rings which came across
De Beer's one hundred million pounds of diamonds.

The music covers them, continues
in the water sunk in every corpse. Beyond,
it has no end except its slow extension
through the musical inflections of the sea.

The Stunt

It came to pass, a motorcycle team's
display of skills and stunts. Loudspeakers said
the plate glass measured half an inch plate-thick,
and as they mounted it on wood for him
angles acutely cut and bit the ground.

The best and youngest rider had reserved
this last trick for himself. Dressed as a clown
he circled on his motorcycle, waiting.
Long multicoloured leg-socks topped his boots.
His baggy shorts blew downwards to his knees.
And also his, the breakable bare chest.
Beneath the dark impenetrable rock –
his helmet, and behind a china vase –
his face, his nerves and toiling muscles moved,
fatigued the vase to fractured alabaster.
His body wrenched, the pale skin on his hands
and fingers tensed to answer, milkshake flesh
turned round and round as to some spirit's call.
He was presiding at a civil war
between his body and the brave ideal
to execute his trick – until he felt
the white truce of his chest. A flight of pulses
butterflew in him, and were exhaled.

He lowered down his visor suddenly
and lit the headlamp as his engine reared
the front wheel high. Now he was coming fast,
and just before he bowed his head to serve,
before he earned his glory, I could see
the intimate and personal sharp twist
of nerves, minute detail transcending one
immensity immediately ahead.

Spectators pressed against the fence, our necks
in treble file, despite our wincing eyes
all of us saw what happened – those of us
who had not turned away. The steel band

of glass on glass and steel crescendoed past
the crashing impact. The rider slumped across
the handlebars in perfect vertigo.

We stood astounded then to see this man
spurning his achievement and ride on.
Supplanting his own courage and his skill
with greater fortitude, he now rode back
towards us at the fence, taunting taut
once more the sinew stretch of muscle
for applause, his limbs to higher triumph,
racking tough determination for the crowd,
for his torrential ego, for himself.

We small men standing by, who navigate
our palms, how could we dare interpret this?
Display of bleeding arms, indelible veins,
his brighter blood inside and through and out,
the gashes opening up like smiling lips.
The pointillistic blood had painted drips
down the idiotic make-up of the clown.
His foolish grin grotesque. His mind bruised
but ignorant of glass. His feat fulfilled
all the more for the reddening grass.

He demanded eyes, and we respect the brave.
The one man stood superior. He waived
his nausea and ours, and was for that short time
undeniably a high god, this man
who only then consented he would have
the pretty bloody glass withdrawn from him,
a tourniquet soaked, and a hospital shocked.

She passed the test. He would not let her drive.

Her rising anger snapped taut.
She angered now for much more
than liberal female thought.
She'd won a pretext. A quick
and bad-tempered thing to score
him, strip of flex, hard plastic,
golden copper-wire core –

she snatched it from his proud car
and looped it round her wrist, rope
to grip in soft palms. So far
she'd only slapped in defence.
She had to make lemon-soap
smooth fingers grip down, go tense
and let him know. She could hope.

He saw her. He started back
and set his rushing mind high.
She advanced. Was that *his* knack
he saw her using? And on
she came towards him, to try.
She dared and sprang at his gone
feet and cracked the flex close by

his smaller bowed head. Cringe-eyed
he flinched aloud at that slap
of air. But he would not hide.
He parried with a short knife.
A white strip fell. The whip-snap
sang by and came back. His wife
brought down the ease of her trap.

He could only move a hand
in shy defence. The sharp flex
cut deeply. The girl could stand
over. She loved this. Loving
what an opened impulse checks,
what a tight-lipped grin could bring,
her freedom loved itself. No checks

for that or anything she might
now do to him. He bent, afraid
to jerk his knife, stand and fight.
She means it, he realised.
He felt the wound she had made.
She'd hurt him! He hadn't sized
her up at all. But he had paid

for all her things, hadn't he?
But the red wire whistled round
again, caught him suddenly.
Her wild mouth was also heard.
He stumbled low at the sound,
but stood. He'd been made absurd,
he knew. He watched the flex wound

less tightly in her tight grip.
The car at his back, he held
his knife up staff-like, a drip
of blood on the shaking skin
at the pointed end. She yelled
like Sioux or Samurai in
pleasure or in pain: he repelled

her. Obsessed by her own sake
she lashed the long wire out,
wrapped the blade and saw him take
her weapon up, away, and twist
it quickly from her. Without
the hard flex her whitened wrist
could not spin her anger out.

Her husband was so surprised
by his success, her next move
beat him. He lost his new-prized
winning knife. She simply kicked
it from his fingers. She wove
her hand in flex again, picked
up the hot knife too, and drove.

33

Jack the Ripper's Message

When I was killing women in discreet
and diverse corners of the city night,
large numbers of compulsive reasons, facts
and motives, gathered from my secret life's
strange influences, met in my cold palms
and worked in all the fingers of my hands.

I have practised murder to the great alarm
of England's people, press and government.
But I've been wondering if I have not placed
my life in danger, not only from the law
but from my own discretion. Thoughts of mine
have been debating on my acts, and have agreed
on resolutions, made complaints against
the terror I have spread throughout this town
and, further, the confusion that I know
has been quick-spun and cocked within my mind
by all my constant training in the use
of will to exercise my grievous crimes.

I ask an urgent meeting to be held
upon this matter of my bloody work
in London's boroughs, and I truly wish
the Secretary luck that he may soon
be able to apply his powers to me.
I sometimes feel I am already lost,
and sentenced to a term of certain fate
(which started after that first one I did)
whose length is equal to the hopeless days
left in my life. Yet, if there's room between
the lynching inclination and the path
of justice – that is, to hang me from a rope
till dead – I'd beg a word of sympathy
upon the grave distress of murderers.

Well, Sir, the task yet lies before your men.
You'll have to find me first, you'll have to smoke
me out. I'm Jack the Ripper, and you know
I'm much too clever, much too hot and quick

to give myself to you without a game.
But I expect the first man who suspects,
from looking at my nervous, frightened eyes,
that I'm the very kind of man to keep
a stock of lethal steel possessions – guns
and pistols, daggers, knives – to tell his tale
of observations to the police. Armed well
with only his defensive truncheon-wood,
a senior officer will then proceed
to where I live, a warrant in his hand,
while rows of constables hold back the mob.

Should I in some last-minute loss of nerve
refuse him entry, then he may abuse
my final piece of private dignity,
break down my door and enter my own house
by day or night under the force of law
and, searching all those places where I still
conceal prime evidence against myself,
seize and detain the various instruments
that he will find. But I shall try to prove
that certain of the weapons that he finds
were not kept for the uses as above
but for the taking of my own poor life,
and I shall fight his conscience to prevent
them passing into his safe custody.

The Cool Season
(for Val Curtis)

Intoxicated, when I first arrived,
by the scenery – still am. Colour-drunk
on the obscenely fertile jungle-green.
Invigorating place, with picturesque
poverty in sight of the English tourists –
or Krauts, who can be found even here.
Myself, I left my camera behind
but *felt* like a tourist, haggling blind
to get an ethnic terracotta jug.
So far, that's the only ethnic thing –
except dead flies – to decorate my room.

The work began at once, establishing
a simple but decent water supply
for the camp – my 2nd Class degree
in Engineering put to use at last.
Nice job – technically not difficult
to build a well, protect a spring, but it's hell
to organise the trucks and the refugees.
They drift in here from everywhere – it seems
there are a dozen dialects. A group
arrived last night, said they had been running
for two years. And there are local people,
frightened from their homes by true stories.
Many *shambas* are deserted now – they're prey
to both sides, soldiers and guerilla squads.
The agencies feed scores of refugees,
it's marvellous, but now the army chiefs
are stopping that – retribution, they claim,
for harbouring guerillas in the camps.
Outside, hundreds starve, surrounded by
plantations – coffee and bananas, maize,
cassava, mangos, groundnuts brought to ruin.

The political arena is disgusting,
worse every day. Reports and rumours talk
of guerilla fire in our area,
so now the government troops have the excuse

to misapply the new emergency
reforms and, drunk out of their minds, or stupid,
they do so all the time. The road blocks
have become extortion centres. They use
the population, everyone, as slaves.
A sniper hits a sentry in the hand:
the army charges in and massacres
a village, careful to drag out a man
rigged up in questionable sniper's clothes –
but no one dares, of course, to question that.

I sometimes visit a clinic in the bush –
sometimes, I say, no more than that, because
it's just unbearable – where there are kids
who will survive with two limbs or less,
and a pregnant woman, a woman five
or six months pregnant, I tell you,
raped thirty times by soldiers.

                    What is there
to do? I listen to the radio –
I am the only one who can pick up
the military wavelength. The clinic,
even our headquarters, may have to be
evacuated soon, and where to then,
when the only safety for the refugees
is having white eyes see what's going on?
And they're quickly catching on to the idea
that capturing or shooting whites and snatching
international relief-work heads
is the only thing that gets publicity –
in fact, the only news the pressmen have
at all. But the radio is quiet tonight,
except for a disc-jockey signing off,
saying any old thing as if he were
already safely home.

              I am in bed –
I'm ill. I am *depressed* with getting ill.
I'd just recovered from a second bout
of malaria – yes, malaria –
when I came down with a stomach bug.

But, amazing! – when asked for a specimen
the diarrhoea went away like magic.
I'm still weak, but with fewer choppy feelings,
and I am unprecedentedly thin –
rib cage and cheekbones discovered! My tan
has faded, so I'm faking it – now all
of me comes out of a secret bottle.

Depressed, too, with the tension and fear.
The unpredictability wears me down.
Depressed, because a priest whose mission-house
I often used to stay at has been shot
by the guerillas. I was with him an hour
before he died – he seemed fine. It's these things
that wear me down. I think a holiday,
a short break in the mountains, is the cure.
And when this job finishes, to find
another one with like minds and ages,
but at the lake shore, in a quiet area.

Thank God the cool season is here. I wish
I could be out. It's really only us,
the SCF, UNICEF and the Red Cross –
a smart set of well-paid Swiss lads –
who make Kampala's nightlife. As you can
imagine, there is a shortage of girls here
so I do fairly well, despite it all,
and it's excellent, moreover, for my French.

The Hen Man

I cut your egg-shaped head
from a piece of clay rolled flat,
stuffed paper bags beneath
to bulge the lips and forehead,
the bits that are going to protrude.

I pierced your ears,
sponged your nose with floor-wax
for a shine, tattooed your cheeks
in human profiles and you smiled –
you liked that.

I gave you teeth of broken toothpicks
blackened with a hell of candle-fire.
I mottled you with iron oxide:
you turned into equatorial wood
and showed me the jeer of a totem man.

I found you in a book of masks
from Papua New Guinea. Hen Man,
I've finished your mutation.
Now do you have your powers? I see
the plaited string is struggling for your hair.

I'm going to hang you in the hall,
with a lightbulb behind your face
to make you seem severe or so.
What do you think you will do up there?
Scare the visitors, will you?

Or pull the spirits from our illnesses,
bring down the drought's-end thunder from the sky?

First Flight

'His thoughts made pockets and the plane buckt.'
JOHN BERRYMAN

I.

I reassured myself, strapped
back in a window-seat, and heard one
humming engine practising. Two Rolls-Royce
turbofans – very powerful, I thought.

Taxiing, a ground-mist swung
around the fuselage. Mist, in shapes
of cables and tarpaulins, made grey
the black bitumen and silver wings.

Acceleration heaved. I had never travelled
so suddenly. Sequences of guiding eyes
lining the runway strained, unfocused, fell
down as the nose-wheel rose.

I was tilted. I felt my stomach
suffer at the whole plane's lift.
While I perspired, what made my air-hostess's
make-up gleam? Her smile of confidence.

Cut by the sharpened sun, cut,
thrown from folding undercarriage,
loops of mist were tumbling in my smooth
airliner's slipstream, apeing its colours.

II.

The plane's bulk shook at the edge of the sea,
as a bather shakes, then bobbed out
on a warm current. I was being flown.
I could be flown, I could! I scanned

the Dover Strait, its harbours, its resorts.
Long streaks, where the wind squalled,

became familiar as my own blue corduroy.
Our twin jets thrust for height – that's good.

Three ferry-boats on Channel crossings sailed
between their ports. They seemed to be all right,
each one pointing to or from the same
white coastline as the arrow of its wake.

But the atmosphere whitened. The glass
was made opaque, and rainfall blurred the view
in the manner of a work by Georges Seurat.
A thundercloud had folded round on us,

had slung across and put its dull shine
on the metal, slipping in between the bolt
and the bolt-hole and quivering the wing span.
It broke our frequencies, translating words,
whole sentences into its private code.

My seat-belt pulled me tight, and tighter still,
the lemon wheel pouring out my drink
over the rim. Our modest fuselage,
behaving like a hull in a bad sea,
pitched in the north-east swell of the air.

Down, a glimpse, as my side
of the plane dipped suddenly.
Is that Paris! Roofs, dark squares,
dark lines: each tiny coloured piece

a fragment. Only the spreading smoke
attempting to arrange itself.
No pattern, only parts,
shapes but no design:

Paris appearing as an old mosaic
upset or shattered, split
through by the Seine
and fissured by black railways.

Clouds removed the sight, by skill.

III.

The storm released our wings.
The ailerons lay still.
The strong air made the plane ascend
and let us have our altitude.

We came up, sent up, through deep clouds
whose moisture sealed behind us,
rainwater forming on small particles
of pollen, dust and salt from earth.

The process spread below us,
an experimental field of gas and liquid
lit and cultivated by the sun,
extending to create an arc-horizon
in suggestion of the planet's curvature.

Rain fell on Earth depressingly,
down from the brilliant white cloud's underside.
A boy in Mansfield wiped – *ah!* – his glasses clean.
But no one else was looking up. The plane,
well-hidden even from the eagle's lens
and from all telescopes, could not be seen.

Removed from tracks on the damp ground,
from contact with the living-room floor,
we were transfering horizontally
towards the distance, into and through
the distance, into another. I could not
see anything but isolating cloud.

I didn't know where I was. How could I know,
when I could not see anything to lend
me balance? There was no one to ask,
there wasn't anyone to listen to.
No landmarks. What could I judge by?
Without proximity of objects, how
could I tell distance in the sky?

I carried in my mind
impressions of an English midland town,

an image for the mind's security.
Impressions of our house, but all its doors,
its picture-rails, walls and window-frames
went changing into blueprint diagrams.
Grass, hedges, plants became short lines,
the garden's size reduced to section, plan
and elevation, scaled down like Paris, flat.

My childhood garden views
returned to me without perspective.
Our climbing-tree's odd branches have become
as simple as a flight of spiral stairs.
I see the opposite corner of a lawn
but not the corner I am climbing in.

I am unhurt now by my father's
hard orchard: not tripping on the rungs,
nor falling from my footholds,
not being bruised, nor bruising the soft fruit,
nor being stung in August at the top.

My blood now passes through,
undirected through its rivers, my throat
no longer thirsty for the green pears,
green apples, when the first bite
inside a sharp-sweet one would really turn
my blood, and dress my hands cut by the bark,
and make the thunderstorm in the afternoon
run off my arms, and the wasp go down.

I don't recall, don't miss the sleep,
the dreams that would follow. Held
in the window seat's wide overview
I can't sleep now, or rest. I'm not
aware of this reclining fabric.
I'm touching nothing, cannot feel the touch
of it or any of my clothes on me,
not feeling less secure without their warmth.

The special, pressurised cabin air
is breathing in my lungs. The mist
that I inhaled has been neutralised
already. I am in an air-conditioning

which neither calms me nor invigorates,
moves without convection, without dew,
without a fragrance or the shock
of mass blossom, nor the equally sweet smell
of ripening and rotting fruit.

The burnt-out, smouldering dead wood,
becoming ash, was still hostile enough
to scorch me. One window-frame
repeatedly inserted both my thumbs
with splinters. But I could dig them out.
Cold water in the bath repelled me,
but it would soon flow out.
Our first dog leapt at me,
but it would soon be trained.

IV.

Now all these childhood enemies of mine
have been outlived by me, that is to say,
succeeded by the victim of adult ones.
Evaporation took away that water.

The orchards fall by fire, or by age,
or age replaces them with natural trees
as the wood-grain, pips and apple leaves
become imprints upon new-forming coal.

Our labrador lies in the present period –
Quaternary – to be exact the Recent
sub-division – head face-down, its open mouth
close to the bigger jawbones of the Pleistocene.

Amoeba, hydra, leave no trace:
but in some other sediments are unknown spores,
pre-mackerel and monsters of the deep,
amphibians' legs, long vermin teeth,
hundreds of identical cows' ribs
from off the prairies, mammoth tusks,
bones of even the smallest animals,
descendants of those dying on the Alpine slopes

below us now, to be interred in screes
and leaf-mulch by the winter;

three skeletons from my grandparents' deaths,
a fourth one from my uncle's sudden death
which even as a child I heard of;
all their bits and pieces put away
amongst the general broken vertebrae
of women, snakes and other men;

the perfectly constructed form
of birds which did know how
but, being servile and illiberal,
would never fly above the highest cloud;

all these remains, all cavities and joints,
disintegrated by the traction-rivers,
dissolving in the chaos on the ocean floor
or, trapped in the faulted strata of old rocks,
jolted, smashed down by the metamorphic earth;

these fossils made to slide around the globe
on continental plates and shelves,
held down forever to a horizontal plane,
mixed up with tools and bricks

as the aircraft flies,
achieving distance from its origen
by flying further on its tangent
in a contrary direction to the world.

V.

The need to build a house and live in it,
leave it in the morning, work hard
in any local place to slot yer purse
with shiny money, and the need
to bring food into it, and beer to drink,
something to sit on while the cigarette
or pen between your fingers thinks of cash
and worries on the problems of your family,
and puts up question marks in hypochondria;

the sex well done, without solemnity,
but the young man's lust for her, or *her*,
another woman or, if possible,
another girl again, was always there,
the fast orgasm panging through my mother's dog
in a wide street: now, no more of that.

No more watching, staring at,
no more listening, tasting, sniffing at,
burning, cutting, bleeding, falling,
having being in the rain.

Now that I don't see, and don't care to be seen,
can't hear anyone, and don't care to be heard,
can't touch anyone, and don't care to be touched,
what do I sense? What can I think?
What can I sense of something new,
new mental talent, new ability,
new bodily emotion for the mind,
something to satisfy and keep me satisfied
beyond the cycle of my strong emotions?

Not sensitivity. I'll use
the arms of chairs no more. I feel
I lack conditions I can call intense.
But what is the secret, please, the secret? –
for nothing has occured to me.
Intensity, not sensitivity,
but nothing has occured to me.
I will not use the arms, the backs of chairs.
My arms, *my* back; and yet I feel I need
much more than mental-physical intensity.
But what, what pulls me down?
What pulls me down? Why gravity?

VI.

It is this pressure, gravity,
with its intenser, constant force
that keeps me down.
It keeps down everything, ensures
that everything fits in its place.

If we move up, even like satellites,
we are eventually returned
by gravity, exhausted.
All of us fit in our places,
and I am one of us, although myself.

Only the slightest gases – hydrogen
and helium – and the special metal parts
from old American spacecraft,
are able to pass through and stay.

The airplane has to cruise, at cruising height,
relying on the points of its design
to carry through its thousand-mile range.
Its kerosene's inflammable,
and having burnt to let me try
the ignorant, brief joy of the flying fish
before the sea regains its stupid eyes,
it burns to bring my first flight down.

The soil in the end eats everything,
takes back everything and anything else,
the casts of earthworms and the men above.
At most, mud takes the soil to a stream,
stream to a river, river to the sea,
the sea to itself and other seas.

At most, bad weather circulates
the numbers of bacteria –
all reproducing fast, or dead, or dying fast
in any cubic measurement
of water, fire, oxygen or soil –
distributes them amongst the atmosphere
and leaves a damp grey film
thickening on the windows of the plane.

Dense layers of strato-cumulus
which never separated land and sea
from the clear air, come up to meet us,
give way and take us in at once.

That soft horizon formed by eight-eighths cloud
must surely be, I realise, a straight line,

arched willingly by the eyeball's optical tricks
to give a false impression to the mind
of surface curvature and, skilfully,
the illusion of good distance gained from it.

The cloud has been a convex lens, then,
of vapour and refracting water drops,
which has magnified a little and diminished,
according to my partial understanding.

For this is what I've gained:
a partial knowledge of my ignorance.
I don't know why the warm sky
appears to be light blue –
I only know the spectrum is involved.

And the wind beneath these turning ailerons?
What is that? There are more mysteries,
but are there no more to be known by me?
The wind is coming from a strange pact,
which I don't understand, between
the temperature and rotation of Milan.

VII.

Icarus with his wings intact,
I'm coming down right now.
Another mist has risen to retrieve.
It's entering the corners of the glass.

The now obsequious airplane
bows before the red and green lights
of navigation. Parallax
restored, parallax enforced.

Below,
a man's back, hunched on the bicycle,
goes riding round the airport's
wide perimeter.

His house moves past
his slow horizon.

The Psychoanalysis of Dr Samuel Johnson as a Volcano

On the far side of the volcano, two
so careful figures quickly probe the ash
with special glass tubes. They may look like two
men of Letters, literary men who flash
about their hobby, but they are in fact
geologists. Their ways are crude. They've come
to whisk away volcanic gas. The act
is swift, and later in the lab they'll run
the gas through special glass filters. Data
soon derived from these analyses
will then explain, thanks to their computer,
the Volcano's behaviour, if they please.

While in a London Institute, a man
in white constructs (theoretical)
a model of the Mountain's inner span.
Next to him a student studies a sample
in-depth with an electron-microscope.
A literary man? No. He is a young
cartographer whose photographs, they hope,
with observations in the field far-flung
will help to demonstrate the Johnsonian
geology, and to compile the maps
so vital to their Johnson-exploration,
and, if they please, to make Johnson collapse.

The Eel Lake

The enlivening chill at eight o'clock
is what takes them out, not the sullen man
walking to the village for the day.
The two old dogs have bobbed down early
from a farm on the hillside and joined him.
One of them, a labrador, he names Chase,
the other, a mongrel, Bonafide.

When the journey changes us
we all might change our name –
like freshwater eels, the snake-fish
born near Bermuda in the Sargasso Sea
which drifts for three years to Europe
as eggs and larvae, undergoing shape
and grey-green colour. A way is found
up river-estuaries, up streams.
They even develop into lakes.

Often fooled and now going blind,
Chase is still first down to the eel lake.
Nothing doing. But they are off again,
noses down, testing everything, excited
by the different things they know are going to come –
horses, horse-sweat, sticks, hooters, children –
bounding up to them or through the air.

Returning at dusk, off the leash
and led by hunger, they trot ahead
towards the calling of their real names
along the known path between the fields
which they have realised a hundred times.

They smack their tongues at water in the bowl
and wander through the kitchen from the back,
or take the other route behind the trees
and in at the front door. They love that,
and they love being grabbed by surprise
or hugged tightly before they circle down
and squint and loll closely for contact.

By the time they are settling into dreaming,
eels may have just been slipped
from the water by compulsion,
and started gliding through the damp grass,
across roads and gardens, to the shore.

They shall be navigating by smell
and fractional increases of fahrenheit,
but pulled by the instinct of the sea's
magnetic field stamped in their genes:
pulled back inside the green Sargasso,
where the cold North Atlantic orbit
they make only once is concluded
as they breed, then die.

Elegy for My Sister

'Let your hand caress
Its texture, size and mass, feel for the gaps
That may be there, the tender buried edges
Held by the earth.'
ANTHONY THWAITE

They shall find you lying. Smile for them
on your back. Humour them, for they shall not
have been ready for this. Under the mud-pack,
your dead face made up as if to chat
them up, to advertise the barest detail
of its features: the line of a slim nose;
a touch of colour on the cheek, a real
iron compound bought from the earth; the eyes,
round shadows of those eyes above a lack
of milkteeth grinning out below that height
of forehead. Your hair has also changed its look –
styles come and go. And they shall guess those great
blue shadows lit a daughter's brighter past
and, knowing neither, know through their own eyes
the looks of your fine mother have been lost,
and recognise you only as a species.

Unearthing this surprising grave, you need
not hesitate. Disturb her slight decay,
her sleep. She, too, would flinch at what has died.
You joke: a twinkle in her Father's eye,
she slept upon the umbilical cord
for nine due months and half as long on earth,
as helpless as her foetus. Grown so scared
down there, she feels dark, colder than her birth.
Now, while she has the chance, she wants to sit up
and sing '…I wonder what you are' – you joke –
'Up above the world, so high.' Look up.
By definition, astral. Did she speak?
Like stars at dawn she died – so reads your tag?
No. You do not deal with thin air. You want
your reason scientific fact. Dig, dig
her cemetery, and wonder why she went.

Give her a hand, come on, and brush her down.
Out with your trowels and measures, follow these
criteria, and get these points down first:
a)   the relation of the length of the torso
     to the stature as a whole,
b)   that of the span of the outstretched arms
     to the stature,
c)   that of the upper limb to the lower limb,
d)   that of the forearm to the upper arm.

Susan, they've rearranged your parts like parts
in some children's game designed to tease
the skill. They've poked and probed through clinging dirt
for signs of damage, handicap or bruise.
Protection: function of the skeleton,
supporting tissue in all vertebrates.
Pelvis protects the embryo in women,
two kidneys, ovaries, assorted chutes,
intestines. And the skull protects the head.
The ribs defend the arteries, red lungs
and vital heart from a physical God.

What have they found? Skull: whole; and flawless grubs.
Pelvis: perfect for your children's children's birth.
A matching set of fixed and floating ribs.
Shocked biceps dislocate your tongue-and-groove,
ball-and-socket architecture, and they can
find nothing wrong with you. They are stuck.
Carbon 14 dating has your dates done
to the instant, and now the diggers pack
your joints in crates, puzzled how you came to lower
yourself from white flesh without blood to white bone
without flesh in soil, through your finest hour,
an average life expectancy too soon.

You went under with your injury intact,
your mark, distinction; blush – what would have been
your mole in an embarrassing dark place,
your own peculiarity unseen.
The plugging of your lifelong haemorrhage
was left to the exhaustion of your blood.

Your blood, your pint fell down it clockwise, down,
it dried itself out, and the crawling earth
dismantled it, the small hole in your heart.

Of what remains, they shall secure the nation.
Your sun: a perspex coffin's hot strip-light
much longer than your spine. In front, a caption
on a plastic plaque, for you lie in state,
highlit for the visitors on baize.
'Baby. Female. 1956.'
A brief address. Curator, add 'The cause
of death unknown.' Anthropologist,
you reassemble her as she was found.
Repeat how some seed falls on stony ground.

Godly Parents

Talking funny and looking funny –
you don't care! You make yourself
your sacrifice. May God help you.
He intended you to be a righteous girl
but you have no will, no will
whatsoever, no integrity.
Let Him judge you.

Come on. Come on Sunday, won't you?
Show us you can become
the complement we want you to be.
It will be a big day, a great day
so we believe. Well? Jane?
We are waiting for an answer
of some sort or another.

Ibiza
(for Maite and for Fletch)

1.

No poisonous animals, no tricky plants.
Civilisations held the soil sacred.
For 400 years the Carthaginians
ferried their illustrious, metropolitan
old people here to die.

That is why spring strawberries taste so sweet.
That is why the olives are so sharp.

2.

Dry grass in its gullet,

cud in its paunch or *rumen*,
and in the *recticulum* or honeycomb,
and through to the *omasum*
and then in the *abomasum* or maw,

produces beautiful goat's milk cheese.

3.

Can you hear that bird on evening-watch
in the junipers near the cliff?
Which bird can it be, do you think,
calling steadily through the silence?

It will make the same sound for hours,
like the plaintive sonar bleeps
emitted by a scanning submarine.
It's confirming its position to itself
at the centre of its song's carry.
What is this bird, the sonar bird?

It is an owl, the owl
who's father to the lighthouse,
who taught the keeper synchrony,

and led him to the knowledge that,
on the darkest night,
he is the only one at the centre.

4.

The sea can finish crewmen, and make
an idiot of those who try alone.

Ask Roger, when you see him.
First a hand, secondly another,
come over the yacht side;
black hair appears, and a pirate's dagger
clenched in wicked, grinning teeth;
then his arms, darker than blind mullet,
pitch him on the deck:
that's Roger, returning from subfari.

5.

He can tell you stories, tales of how
the Phoenicians left their huge necropolis
and their sea around Ibiza full of figures,
simple baked shapes of men and women
made as offerings to high divinities,
especially to the lovely goddess Tanit,
the most beneficial and the best.

But who is that bird-faced little man
in the tourism promotion poster?
What could he represent but lust?
Was he really welcomed by Tanit
with his necklace and beaky nose,
his barrel-body and long, thin arms
reaching down to a small erection?

6.

A more recent little visitor
was Alfonso XIII, King of Spain.
He called at Portinatx in '29.

The ship moored in the turquoise cove,
the king moored on the shaded deck
resting from war-game manoeuvres.

Or was he there to gather kindling wood
from the pine shore? Perhaps
he was looking for salt, too
(at the wrong end of the island).

Was anyone there to witness him?
Were there no fishermen, no fishwives,
to offer up *merluza a la plancha*?

Probably not – the hungry king
would not have seen a single house.
I should think he folded up
his telescope, and sailed away next day.

Yet the place was called King's Portinatx,
at least for a while, it seems –
until Alfonso was forgotten
by the scared men behind the trees.

7.

When you leave this island
in the spring, what you remember
just as much as the soft, square lines
of the white cottages,

are masses of yellow and some red flowers
in tall grass in a field of trees.

8.

It would be a typical Ibizan house,
dropped centuries ago from a white cloud
to the ground, where it set
in rounded corners and small, square windows;

around it, 700 fig and almond trees,
a few dry sheep and a shallow well;

58

good produce sent to Carthage, Athens and Rome
in amphoras, and plundered for its fame.

But the owner's been bought out.
The new man has installed a row
of solar panels for his energy;
the foundations of a swimming pool are done.

But then, if any well-dressed foreigner
drove up to *your* front door
with millions of pesetas in his fist,
and offered you a foreign cigarette

with kindness, wouldn't you at least
invite him in, and give him a glass of *Hierbas*?
And would you care that figs from here
had once made Pliny eulogise?

9.

And there is the other sort of tourism –
the independent boys and girls
who come with the two red S's in their eyes:
one for cash with two lines through it,
one for sex with numbers in it.

'I learnt to play the Spanish guitar
to make the women love me at parties.'

The islanders are head-shaking sorry:
'We are disagree with your comportment…'

10.

It was different in my father's time.
He told me how he never met a girl –
had scarcely thought about his parents in the night –
until his curiosity reached sixteen.
He went then, with his name Feliciano,
authorised to join the Festeig.
He took the long way there, rehearsing lines and graces
to favour him in her father's sitting room.

Maria Rosa occupied the central chair.
Feliciano, seated with the other boys
in a line on one side, spoke nicely
with the family who'd invited him.
His real thoughts were cleanly dressed
and buttoned close. One by one the young men
went over to a chair placed by her side,
and there talked keenly with the pleasant girl
who, going through the burden of it all,
spoke pleasantly to each of them.
Feliciano, waiting his turn impatiently,
sat watching the direction of her eyes,
their destination. The alloted time was up:
he warned the boy by tossing one small stone,
as was the custom. Still the boy continued.
He threw another stone, harder. Then
the young macho Iberico in him –
in both of them – broke out. A fight
ensued disgracefully outside the house
and Feliciano, in his first Festeig, lost.
Annoying the girl he'd lusted for,
he drew a pocket pistol from his belt
and shot it at the ground before her feet.
She tried to show she wasn't afraid,
but as she *was* afraid he showed disdain
by sounding off his gun at the girl's back,
and swore her and her family Good Night, Goodbye.

Later, his sister asked him how he felt
about the girl. He felt sold, he said.
The ban they placed on him would last for months.
And after many Festeigs, the young
girl's mother chose the one she liked –
a lad who hadn't thrown the warning stones.
Maria Rosa soon appeared at mass
on public Sunday, with her fingers full of rings,
with a key and a heart in chains.

11.

The church of San Rafael
has landed, on its buttresses.

It's like a squatting insect.
It's like a big, albino grasshopper
with its knees sticking out.

12.

I don't see why the Catholics,
long-living in a land like this,
can never be quite sure until they die
that grace has long been granted.

13.

Salt weather made an extract of the cliffs
called sand; blonde people came to holiday
just where the sand accumulated best.
The two-foot Mediterranean tide
was hired as an agent, and the scatty beach
grew up with kleptomania,
becoming rich through centuries of use,
concealing terracotta, hiding one
and five peseta coins, mislaying gold
engagement rings, refusing to yield up
the remnants of a metal detector.

One night, in a vast spectacular
the lighthouse could not follow,
storm-winds screamed up to an octave
that has never been discovered since,
and crashed with Geiger's tremors
from an earthquake in Algeria.
The beach and all its treasure disappeared.
No more people came – until
a circle of men with money sunk in tourism
had new sand made from limestone quarries – coarse,
but fine enough for postcards, and the doctored print
confirming that the sea's strong shade of blue
is the same as in your Saxon-Scandinavian eye.

14.

Pale English girl in pink shorts,
your fat thighs burnt by the sun –
it looks as if the pink has run!

15.

She was flipping through a paper
which I picked up when she'd gone in with the sun,
noticing a small advertisement:

there is a great monster in his stomach,
feeding on a strange, unstable diet;
sour milk, bad vegetables, off meat,
sometimes nothing in particular
will make it angry, and sometimes
no food at all; it kicks the walls
of its cave, and bangs with its fists;

with his stomach's monster thrashing
for a feast of staple rice, this poor boy
is obliged to suffer and lie down;
he either starves a little more
or trusts in foods of appeasement –
parcels from the readers of this tabloid,
who have missed the ad. and only read
the girl page blowing round the topless beach.

16.

Cicadas buzz electrically in the pines,
preparing them to be good telephone poles.

Then once in every fifty years
they buzz like chain-saws.

17.

It is good to see the road they styled
already breaking up, but you can still drive down
to the hotel of their speculative dreams.

When they abandoned it, the wooden props
and scaffolding were spiralled over the cliff;
they have never been washed out,
but washed up and down by winter tides
and twisted into driftwood, or smoothed to forms,
or bitten into terrible animal faces.

The crazy woman who lives in a room of cement
believes herself to be the guardian
of 'the Works'. She's hauled some pieces back
for furniture. She could use the planks
for boarding up her unfinished windows.

Or she could spend her saner days
in taking down the superstructure,
ramming it with her Citroen stuck in reverse,
brakes gone, throwing breeze-blocks
and pushing iron girders over the edge.

Then let wild sage and thyme
in the children's pool be rained on, pines
with roots in the concrete floors helped,
and the setting will be well again, unsaddened.

18.

It's the setting that you go for, isn't it?
'Look,' you say, 'there's one, by the roadside,
under a locust-tree, picking locust beans,
and she's even wearing island costume!'
You are getting out your camera.

But how should you approach her?
It seems ridiculous to ask permission,
ask her to look up and be still;
false to bayonet your tele-photo lens
to close in on her back, broken by work.
That isn't how you want to contact her.

No, you should do it with an ordinary lens,
and you should not have her smile developed
unless you meet her with your proper eye.

19.

And those who come by here
to ride their sentiments and set them
on my lambs, all think like this:

Up here I feel I almost know
God's tears are weeping down in awe
upon this paradise, and each touch
of wind comes breathing my soul's search
gently here to rest...

For those who come by here
to envy me and my environment's
green richnesses, I point out twenty strains
of sun-burnt grass. I know the Latin name
of every plural one. The point is this:
their fresh air yields my dearth, as it were.
It cultivates arthritis. Doors
of the Fiat 127 leave me cold;
people wonder, when I say socialise
with the dew, with debit and alliterative dust.

At evening, I roll out the clouds
that they call harbingers of rain,
and I laugh at the brave sheep
taxiing downwind with crass Icarian ideals
lacking only wings and wax.

20.

Do you remember the Fiesta
of the Full Moon? At the end,
dark rain secured our fires to the beach –
we had to run beneath the bar's cane roof.

We watched the old moon and the clouds
playing at lights for us above,
and lightning blazed in the east
like old artillery, then ceased.

And while the sun was still shining off the moon,
I saw what the dawn does to colours,
and understood then how the painter
only by candle-light
found Prussian blue in the hills.

21.

We are at the summer's end.
As always, I heap the season's rubbish,
sprinkle it with petrol and set fire.
The wind it letting loose the flames
and sending sparks out dangerously.

Do not stare at it; that's melancholy.
It's raining now, but you want to throw
buckets of water on the bonfire,
don't you, and run behind each spark
as if they were your going memories.

22.

The lizards are lying dead still
in the stone walls or disappearing –
private detectives watching us.

You should hire one, the quickest one,
to follow up the clues left by your dreams
this autumn, and contact you in code
from all the places where you will have been,
so that he could always find you.

E

A Man in the Park
(for, and after, Mick)

You could call me dead
I am so still, yet here I am
ostensibly taking the sun in Moor Park,
my jacket ruined for a cushion
but the money and credit cards unstolen –
I checked. I found my shirt and tie
very neatly folded on my left,
after some time. They had even placed
a paperback crime in my hand.

Wasn't I in the drive?
I am sure I was, and then I...
but this killing headache crashes in
and my eyes hurt every time
I try to remember. I had shut
the back door, I was going to the garage
is all I know. And I was being pulled
downwards, down, and fell. I am still
choking on a taste left in my mouth.

They came up from behind
like villains, I suppose, having watched me
hurry my breakfast from the garden.
A cloth was stuffed over my nose,
I sneezed, my eyes stung and withdrew
and could not tell me what or how much
I drank. They made me swallow
but I struggled and some of it did spill
forensic evidence in my hair.

Too dizzy for interpreting my watch,
I did not wake up until, when –
late afternoon? I must have been
lying here for...all day, I realised.
They must have brought me to the park
and arranged me in this fashion, mustn't they,
although I am curled on my side now –
it blunts these stomach pains, and my neck
will stiffen and lock if I do not move.

They tried to poison me!
Who did? They tried to poison me
and there was not enough! It has worn off
while I have been sunbathing on the grass.
I would say that was clever, that was smart
to leave me here if I knew *why*
they did it. Were they the men I fired
yesterday? Am I being watched?
Or searched for, I hope.

I can't stand up. I have not lain down
with so much free time in this park
on a Thursday since I used to play
truant from Metalwork. The same girls,
perhaps, are browning for the year,
I can hear them. None are in the hollow
I seem to have for myself. If I raised
my arms and they noticed, they would think
it was someone waking up, able to speak.

A little boy approached me cautiously
with a stick. He was called away
by his mother, but Mozart overtured
the coming of ice-cream for him. He took
the 50p I held up, and stole back
brandishing a can of fizz. It was no good,
he had to open it for me. I tipped the change
back in his hand, and he tore off
with a secret he would never tell.

It's almost five. The girls have packed. They cross close
but nobody is going to glance long enough
to stop. The only thing coming near
is that dog again – dogs and children know
when something is wrong – and the shadow of the trees
reaching me. I ought to crawl there
and lean around one. I would be seen, and may
be understood. To make manoeuvres then,
swaying like a twelve-day kitten.

Trees before me, now beside me,
and now, now I've got one. It's a beech.
I am trying to hold on, and I can.

There is a shed: the warden is over there.
I shall head off across the cricket pitch
with the sun plunging through my sight
towards him. I am setting off but no,
wait, my legs just won't, they do no more
than fold and set me down.

La Plaza de San Felipe Neri, Barcelona

When I lost my way,
I came across the Plaza Neri –
more like a courtyard than a square.
On one side, a church whose walls
are shot away, pitted, at the average height
of full-grown male chests.

A football
bangs against the masonry,
dislodging bullets. Sharp recoil
of point-blank sub-machine guns,
succeeded by the rebound
of a well-struck kick for goal.

The square is full of whooping boys.
They're playing on their fathers' graves;
at school they're learning history;
and the eldest sons of the dead
are guarding barracks, armouries, and the King.
It was for them the Civil War was fought.

Skiing Holiday in Italy

Every frost prepares the rock
with the colour of snow and ice.
Every rainfall sinks in the fractures
and makes the minerals soluble.

Every heavy snowstorm
splits the limestone,
loosens and removes the Dolomites
with an axe of freezing water.

How we managed to stay upright,
with the ageing mountain moving under us,
I'll never know. But we learnt to ski
despite the stress of geological time,

controlling our legs as we could,
keeping the pine trees vertical,
our bright ski-fashions speckled down the white slopes
in the cold, dry, exhilarating air.

On New Year's Eve, our last day,
an Italian flew down close to us,
carried in the talons of a great hang glider of prey,
and we *still* stayed on our feet.

That evening, we all transfered our balance
to the discoteque. We danced with Disney animation,
with our watches synchronised, and when the bells
broke out, then midnight was confirmed,

we knew the year had switched,
and someone passed around some sweet champagne,
Lucia dipped her tongue between my lips,
streamers and things were flung up in the noise.

In the high valley no clocks,
no minutes but the earth's
and atmosphere's mechanism
caused an avalanche, remote and unobserved.

Metaxa Brandy
Sonnets for Maria

> '*The logic of all beauty is surprise,*
> *The reason of all love the unseen end.*'
> WILFRED SCAWEN BLUNT

The Bus to Athens

Eleven travelling on a coach, ten
are foreign, one of whom at Camden Town
on our departure found me, too, alone
and took her biased choice among the men
for company and more in three whole days
of journeying, perhaps to last beyond,
we'll have to see, as sleeping we grow fond
on the narrow seats, while our dream delays.

She inspires the infatuous. She weans
my crossed imagination to assume
that I foresee her radiance in jeans
in perigee, her eyes on future nights
like conspicuous moons or satellites
of old Uranus silvering a room.

Greek

Brought up Orthodox, not let out with men
until nineteen, with the principle 'my life,
my body is my own' (to be a wife)
she toured the States. One of her several men
stayed two months: married at a friend's place
in Florida, he flew for the U.S.
Air Force and she soured, nursing less and less
her husband's junk-food alcoholic case.

They had no kids – she wanted none. He gave
500 dollars when, two years gone by,
she ran back to Europe, back, full of why
the Church School urged the tall girls to behave –
her older single sister's point of view.
The best man had whispered, 'He's no good for you.'

Sad Yugoslavia

They stoop low, doubled in the rows, and choose
to ignore us, or they walk their rutted tracks
beside the only road, which they don't use.
A line of backs all buff and bunched like sacks
of market produce.

              Later, in a bout
of rain, we stopped, surrounded by the year's
subsistence, helpless with our fuel run out.
We heard shouting, a sound of crashing gears
across the plain: a decrepit lorry piled
with beet. It pulled up, concerned and careful.
The men consulted, watched us smoke and stub
our cigarettes. Exchanged for Dunhill Mild,
we siphoned diesel by the bucketful
and pissed beyond the headlights in the scrub.

To Go Out

Seducing some is off: they'll have no fun,
not knowing what seduction is about,
who've not been in a pub or scarcely out,
have no bed and don't intend to get one.

Frowning, as you down Metaxa brandy,
for vanity I boast this, not for you,
ashamed to realise that it was you
who met me and seduced – that you might be,

tempter of ridiculous decorum,
my customer: 'Do you want to go out
with me?' If so, I'm like the girl with eyes
played wide behind the bar and in no doubt
who 'What – what do you mean, go out?' replies
in wonderful, feigned and cautious wisdom.

Aphrodite's Daughter

Once she slips beneath I brush back her hair
and know to get her foreflesh. Science has shone
her curves I caress. This way I am gone
to where she seethes and crowns below my flair,
as Aphrodite on a scallop shell
enraptured by the rhythm of the wind.
The shore of Cyprus, now these sheets, had sinned
in capturing you. There your freedom fell.

Which is to say that we, mindful of sex,
expect ourselves. I bite into your mouth,
into. Back you bite. Now, here, where you flex,
are fission, fusion, fission after fission –
sides of the heart implode then, and the berth
flutters in fulfilment and in ions.

Heroic Love Song

Devices borne on the shields of heroes
I find manifest in you, who have led
the pre-heraldic history of those
crested helmets to the destined spearhead
of the English forces. Let us be allies
in the field, esteemed by our supporters,
and in our charges steeled by our ties.
Let us be emblazoned in our quarters.

In our liveries, bars of white and blue,
and red, white and blue asserting virtue
and high courage, we shall advance, *recte
et suaviter* – the aphoristic way
of precedence adopted for our front:
chevron with heraldic lions rampant.

Bitten

Playing a grape-game, this lithe girl and I,
we would choose a luscious one, consume
the shape together, push it up each warm
slow tongue, through our teeth, then suck at a sly
bursting of soft fruit, juice in a French kiss
whose flavour soured when I tasted my lip
cut, bitten open. Her tongue began to sip
the young blood, lithe girl, lick clean with a kiss

where claws have scratched but now retract from flesh.
So feline. She dilates her eyes like cats
in dark rooms and runs between my legs. No pain:

while in the girls without concern are cats
who would regard the bleeding of my flesh
as flavour for the marrow of the bone.

Confidence Tricks

A Sunday afternoon. The cable-car
rolled up the Capital, the central hill.
Photographers, once we had got that far,
seized us. Persuasive, commercial – 'Hold still!'

Presumed the charming couple then, we stood
in sandals, Polaroids, with smiles to clutch.
Athens in her coracle of hills would,
of course, serve for background. We paid too much.

These we deserve – two copies each of two
insipid black-and-white snapshots: a view
of dummy lovers posing badly, whose

true photochromic lenses stained the gleam
of Athens' white apartments, exposed a steam
of yellow mist above the avenues.

Letter Home

You wish to have described the gorgeous sun,
famous when it sets across the sea –
the Adriatic, from Corfu observed and won
in summer? Why, I cannot say. You see,
there are more than two hundred words to cite:
two hundred starting with 'gl...' alone
pertaining to the quality of light.
No words can let you know the sunset's tone.

You yourself must come, see how you please
these agitated waters at your feet,
these remnants of the moon-ran swell which pleat
upon, upon, and into – on which one sees
the splitting beam at evening, dipped light,
before the colours darken, merge with the night.

On the Beach at Sounion

Finding room for towels, down we go and try
to read or watch phosphene. But pointlessly
we soon start to argue, each upset, and lie
in anger; then oil ourselves.

                            Into the sea –
floundering about below the stark, staid,
surf-white headland temple of Poseidon,
sea-god who extends beyond his colonnade
control. Dropped in the ocean by pagan
providence we swim, we dive and surface
in our vagaries, confounded by gales,
fathoms, shallows, tide, shoal: as mammals crude
or dumb who splash, and who if not pursued
and caught will find that on a beach there's space
for everyone beside the stranded whales.

A Projection on Aegina

A streamlined hydrofoil's stern-wake, cleft
like shavings off a yellow pencil, brought
us from the mainland harbour here in sport
for privacy and fantasy, and left.

We rest beneath an olive grove, a dome.
Late afternoon, inside an hemisphere.
Curved in like longitude short treetrunks rear,
enclosing us, muffling the wash of foam
along the beach. Those twigs and branches, wakes
of silent ships drawn on a globe. Wasp-holes
in ripe or rotting olives, ports of call.

Desire for special private boundaries makes
our fingers compasses, contrives them tall.
We sail in central love between the poles.

An Inclination South

From the last place I left I come to call.
I'm restless, with an inclination south –
to go from the same room, and from your mouth,
inevitably to lose another girl.

Your settled hair kneels on my lap. Strong sea-
swell speaks for me – Aegean would recite…
I should breathe slower in our final night,
lie still as your slow eyes.

                                    But turn to me,
your opened lips are moistened by the sheen
of harbour lights and glisten in the ways
and shape of diamonds on the cards we dealt
face up.

            Maria, love, I never felt
until this time, and never since have felt,
content within the passage of my days.

Estranged Girl

Someone stopped and asked you in the street.
The Greeks don't recognise you – don't chew gum
here in your severed native city's heat.
They have dark hair. You hated them, and left home.

Until I see your Western looks again
(soon, at Swiss Cottage) you will have to walk
pestered by boys and drinkers and those men
who lean up on the toxic air and hawk.

When a waiter asks you, 'Are you English?'
prefer to speak East Coast American;
with that Greek accent fool the Manhattan
Café. Be alien. Don't order fish
or pitta, local stuff. Show evidence
of London, Tampa, foreign residence.

Reunion

In these addictive hours I relapse
from reading up that heavy syllabus
and see your eyes again. I opt for us –
the false displaced enlightenment, the flaps
of paperback-philosophy replaced
at once by your sensations.

                              Bonfire night,
outside in Hampstead. I would set alight
and burn my gasping sacred textbooks, faced
by the chance of lebensraum.

                              For it is you
who opens out my fitted mind. You stand
against the window, you my sultry tanned
model, trying on from some expensive shop
and slowly taking off again your blue
London underwear, fireworks a backdrop.

Leaving Off

Affections in retention, tenderness,
or something else – 'I love you' really meant
for a long time: so that we'll never guess
the depth of one flirtation. Sentiment
belies the risks we chose. (You do not go
with child, my picaresque Moll Flanders: things
are safe). You'll write to me, addressed Ago –
more frequently if recollection clings.

Now disappear. You must. Go now. We must
accept the reservation of your flight,
a losing husband sitting up for you,
your unexpected kind return. Renew
his weaker love and, please, reserve the right
not to remember our engrossing lust.

Souvenirs

With gifts of pomegranate – one, a bag
of Grecian tea, a cotton shirt, I left;
three bars of greensoap in another bag
and one 500 drachma note, I left.

I hid the money, kept the fruit till bad,
folded a shirt too fine to wear. My tea,
a balsam herb. – In soap, I felt I had
a brief elixir dark in alchemy.

What can I give, transmute for her in quid
pro quo, for a personal belonging
of us both, a permanent precious thing
she bought me? – an X carat signet ring
which I –

             I damn near dropped, mislaid or hid/
forgot somewhere, Lost Property (– then did).

Intensive Study

I'm sleeping with a character called Book,
researching her in braille and never cease
to read. I quiver at her frontispiece,
assess her contents. Curling pages – look
at them – part on the right. Her vellum feels
like skin, her skin like vellum, skin so fine.
My fingers bend her legs back to the spine,
fingertips smooth her gutter till she reels:

a climax of conceit. I only touch
her. Book lies unrequited when I leave,
her fearful student. Book, a whore as such
(much less attractive than her paper sleeve),
confirms that passion's in the Greek girl's heart,
and Book's usurped her now that we're apart.

Fruit Bowl

The apple of the eye
soon saw the peaches, and that fig leaf.

The apple had a green skin.
Ideas from Eden formed its core.

One day the cold, gooseberry skin went hot:
the crazymad banana of the phallus
peeled back its skin
and split the fig taboo.

And there I was!...
born in a world
of fruit association:

the sour apple, sour Puritan eye,
the dangers of the fig leaf,
the threat of grapes in hospital.

And then, one day, those tennis strawberries,
oranges of real and abstract goodness,
the mad banana peeling back its skin.